MW00341913

THE

RETIREMENT
PLANNING
MADE EASY

WORKBOOK

A WORKING COMPANION GUIDE TO
RETIREMENT PLANNING MADE EASY
LEADING YOU STEP BY STEP THROUGH UNDERSTANDING,
PLANNING FOR AND PROTECTING YOUR RETIREMENT INCOME

DIANE MARRA, RFC

Copyright © 2016 Diane Marra All rights reserved.
ISBN: 978-0-9972217-1-8

Limits of Liability and Disclaimer of Warranty
The authors and publisher shall not be liable for your misuse of this material.
This book is strictly for informational and educational purposes.

TABLE OF CONTENTS

"FINANCIAL LITERACY IS AN ISSUE THAT SHOULD COMMAND OUR ATTENTION BECAUSE MANY AMERICANS ARE NOT ADEQUATELY ORGANIZING FINANCES FOR THEIR EDUCATION, HEALTHCARE AND RETIREMENT." – *RON LEWIS*

INTRODUCTION

Retirement Planning Made Easy was designed to educate you about an approach to retirement income planning that differs from the dated, one-size-fits-all philosophies that can all too often put you, your money, and your family at risk. It offers a blueprint for planning a safer, more secure, low-risk retirement.

The book is intended to explain retirement income as distinct from other kinds of investing; inform you about important tips and potential pitfalls; provide a solid base of knowledge about the retirement income landscape; empower you to take ownership of your retirement income planning; and support you in choosing the right professionals to help with this process.

Even though I recommend finding an advisor to work with as you begin assembling your retirement portfolio, I also advocate for you to be a well-educated consumer who can participate in the process with intelligence and awareness. You don't have to be an expert, but you can be prepared to evaluate the professionals and their strategies, do your due diligence, and make the right choices for yourself.

As you learned in the book, much of the planning process requires you to contemplate and answer important questions—from emotional ones about your life, plans, and risk tolerance to practical ones about your financial position and health, among others. Some of the process also requires you to gather information that you and the advisor will need to properly plan and execute your strategy.

As I wrote the book, I realized that it would be helpful for many readers to address all these questions, reflections and information-gathering in a structured manner. That's why I developed this companion workbook. Chapter by chapter, it consolidates the essentials from each section of the book, and leads you through the process of answering the key questions. It will literally help you "fill in all the blanks."

When you begin working with a financial advisor you trust, you'll find it infinitely more productive if you have organized your answers and material. This workbook will help you do so—efficiently and completely. When you have done your part, the advisor will better be able to do his/hers (and will no doubt be pleasantly surprised to discover you're so well-prepared).

Use this workbook to personalize and fill in the vitals you learned about in the book, and start to optimize the money that you have—for the life that you want in retirement.

To the retirement of your dreams!

- Diane Marra

CHAPTER ONE

KEYS TO A SUCCESSFUL RETIREMENT INCOME STRATEGY

IMPORTANT IDEAS

KEY CHAPTER TAKEAWAYS—SUMMARY

IN CHAPTER ONE, WE LEARNED:

● **The state of retirement income planning is in flux and the landscape has changed.** Employer retirement plans are a thing of the past. Social Security may be uncertain. More than ever before, retirees are dependent upon their investments to generate a consistent and secure retirement income.

● **It's your responsibility to seek out a reliable strategy that will suit your needs.** Educate yourself enough to understand and take control of your retirement income, even if you have help. Your success will depend on your own involvement as well as that of the advisor you choose to work with.

● **There's no such thing as too much planning.** Not planning for eventualities can lead to income shortfall. Thinking your retirement income is enough, and strategically planning for it to be enough, are two different things.

● **Don't allow your portfolio to retain high-risk investments.** Losses can significantly reduce your income and devastate your retirement. You can take less risk and still do very well in retirement.

● **The accumulation phase and the distribution phase of retirement planning are entirely different,** requiring different strategies and different mindsets. What you earn on your money (return) is secondary once you enter retirement. What is primary is the safety, security and preservation of the assets that will generate your income streams.

- Inflation, market fluctuations, unstable investments, expensive health care, long-term care, inflation, tax changes and the state of the economy as well as longevity are all significant factors to account for when structuring your retirement plan.

- **Be proactive about the hows and the whys of your portfolio design.** People often have no idea how or why their current portfolio was constructed and invested the way it is. Most people don't want to invest their life savings in a highly volatile stock market, but do so on the advice of brokers.

- Choose an advisor who is well-versed in the distribution phase of retirement.

HOW DO I MAKE THE MOST OF THIS CHAPTER'S ESSENTIALS?

1. Find an advisor:

It is certainly possible to do a great job of planning on your own if you have the depth of knowledge. However, for most people the safe choice is to enlist the help of a qualified retirement income advisor who specializes in retirement income planning. I suggest you find an advisor to work alongside you as you begin piecing together your retirement portfolio to secure your future.

Use these steps to move through the process of finding the right advisor:

THINGS TO DO

Get names of recommendations from friends, relatives, and advisors you trust in other fields.

NAME	PHONE	EMAIL
_____	_____	_____
_____	_____	_____
_____	_____	_____
_____	_____	_____
_____	_____	_____

Read the websites of the recommended advisors.
Make any notes about pluses or concerns here.

NAME	NOTES
_____	_____
_____	_____
_____	_____
_____	_____

Contact those whose philosophies and presentation instill confidence and comfort.

NAME	PHONE	EMAIL
_____	_____	_____
_____	_____	_____
_____	_____	_____
_____	_____	_____

Set up one or two preliminary meetings.

NAME	DATE
_____	_____
_____	_____

2. Interview the Advisor:

QUESTIONS TO ASK

● What does this advisor consider to be his or her specialty or specialties? Where does his or her experience lie?

_____

_____

_____

● Does the advisor know the difference between the accumulation phase and the distribution phase of retirement planning? Does he or she focus on or specialize in the distribution phase?

_____

● Does the advisor have favorite instruments or investments? Does he or she focus on only one or two products, or offer access to a wide range of options?

_____

_____

● Are there any options, instruments or investments the advisor is negative about or refuses to work with?

_____

_____

● What does the advisor say about risk?

_____

_____

● Will the advisor conduct a series of strategy sessions with you to find out who you are, what you want to accomplish, and where you want to end up?

_____

● Will the advisor analyze your particular Social Security scenario and base recommendations on this individualized assessment? _____

● Will the advisor monitor your progress and your portfolio for you?
● How closely and how often will the advisor be in touch?

_____

_____

● Will the advisor keep you abreast of any opportunities that arise, or risks that need to be managed?

_____

● Is the advisor focused on maintaining the integrity of your retirement capital at all times?

_____

What are the rates or fees involved, and what is included?

_____

_____

_____

NOTE: On page 25, there are more questions you can bring with you to your meeting.

 THINK ABOUT...

3. Pledge to Take Responsibility for your Plan

I UNDERSTAND AND PLEDGE THAT:

❏ I will get the help I need, but I will not hand the whole process off to someone else.
❏ I will learn how and why my portfolio is designed the way it is.
❏ I will educate myself so that I can be aware and conversant in discussing all pertinent isues with my advisor.

THINK ABOUT...

4. Review the Risk Factors

There are five key risks associated with retirement income that you can account for in your planning (PUBLIC POLICY CHANGES are a sixth entirely beyond our control). To correctly and adequately plan your retirement, these risk factors must be considered and accounted. Not doing so can lead to the erosion of your retirement capital, which in turn will impact the amount you live on each month.

LONGEVITY In our age of advanced medicine, retirements are getting longer. At one time, many people didn't last long after the typical retirement age of 65. Now many do. Retirement today can stretch upwards of 30 years. How likely this is for you depends on many factors. There are no guarantees, but consider your likelihood of living 10, 20, 30, 40 years beyond retirement (and discuss with your planner). Some factors to consider include:

AGE OF MOTHER AT DEATH	_____	SMOKER/NONSMOKER?	_____
AGE OF FATHER AT DEATH	_____	DRINKER/NON-DRINKER?	_____
SIBLINGS AGES OF AGES AT DEATH	_____	HEALTHY DIET?	_____
PAST SERIOUS ILLNESSES	_____	REGULAR EXERCISE?	_____

INFLATION Inflation can cause your annual income needs to skyrocket, and can devastate your retirement over time. Plan for it or you will be subject to dwindling income amounts as your portfolio does not correctly adjust to inflation.

I WILL PLAN FOR _____% INFLATION BY: _____

HEALTHCARE EXPENSES Healthcare is one of most older adults' largest expenses. One study from the Employee Benefit Research Institute recommends having $227,000 for medical expenses per couple in retirement. My experience with my own clients suggests it can be quite a bit higher.

I expect to need _____ for my healthcare in retirement.

I expect to need _____ for my spouse's healthcare in retirement.

FLUCTUATIONS Poor market performance will negatively impact your portfolio as well as your income. It can take years upon years just to get back to even, while you're faced with taking a higher percentage of income from a smaller portfolio.

I will restructure for less risk by: _____

TAXES When taxes go up, your income goes down.

I will account for tax increases by: _____

CHAPTER TWO

RETIREMENT INCOME PLANNING

IMPORTANT IDEAS

KEY CHAPTER TAKEAWAYS—SUMMARY

IN CHAPTER TWO, WE LEARNED:

- **The main goal of "income" planning** is to transition your capital into monthly "income" (replacing your paycheck) that you can count on for the rest of your life.

- **You will need have an Income Distribution Plan designed, constructed and implemented.** You can do this yourself if you possess the financial knowledge and experience. If you don't, seek a financial advisor who is experienced in income distribution planning.

- **You will need to analyze your risk tolerance**—how much risk is prudent for your particular situation, as well as your personal tolerance level.

- **You will need to ask yourself a series of questions, related to a range of factors,** that will familiarize you with the work that needs to be done to design your retirement income portfolio. By knowing, answering, and then discussing the right questions with a financial advisor, you can streamline your plan to suit your lifestyle, avoid risk, and capitalize on opportunities.

- A competent financial advisor should conduct a series of strategy sessions with you to fully understand your goals. The advisor needs to know who you are, what you want to accomplish, and where you want to end up.

- Your progress should be monitored—by you *and* your financial advisor. Make sure your advisor agrees to keep you abreast of opportunities and risks in a timely manner. The integrity of your retirement capital is always the chief and ultimate concern in this monitoring.

HOW DO I MAKE THE MOST OF THIS CHAPTER'S ESSENTIALS?

Before you visit your chosen advisor, ask yourself these important questions to acquaint yourself with the issues that need to be addressed. if you don't know all the answers, don't worry—you're not alone. It's your advisor's job to help you with these questions. Together, you and your advisor should be able to answer them by talking and reviewing the financial material you will bring to the table (which we'll cover later). First, fill in as much as you can. How much do you know? What can you learn?

QUESTIONS TO ASK

1. Financial Questions to Start the Process:

● How long would your money last if you had to stop working today, invest your savings, and maintain your current living standards?

_____

● Do you know of any Social Security strategies that will maximize the lifetime benefit for you and your spouse?

_____

● Do you know how to build a retirement portfolio that is designed to create low risk and low volatility?

_____
_____

● Do you know how big of a nest egg you will need as you enter retirement, keeping in mind that you might be retired for 20, 30 even 40 years?

_____
_____

- Do you know about how much you can spend each month if you want your savings to last for the rest of your life?

_____

- What percentage of your pre-retirement income will it take to allow you to maintain your current standard of living in retirement?

_____

- How might the rising cost of health care impact your retirement income plan? Consider any health risks or existing conditions.

_____

- If you have a retirement shortfall, do you know how big it is and what can be done about it?

_____

- Do you understand the proper and most tax-efficient ways to leave a financial legacy to heirs?

_____

- Taking all of this into account, do you know if your retirement income plan is sustainable?

_____

Do your best to reflect on and answer these questions. Again, if you don't know all the answers, don't worry. It's part of the process to discover what you know and don't know, so you can remedy any gaps. If you discover a "knowledge and strategy gap," a good advisor will help. But reviewing these questions will help you better prepare to work with your advisor.

2. Based on these questions, my top concerns are:

1. _____

2. _____

3. _____

4. _____

5. _____

RETIREMENT IS LIKE A LONG VACATION IN LAS VEGAS. THE GOAL IS TO ENJOY IT THE FULLEST, BUT NOT SO FULLY THAT YOU RUN OUT OF MONEY.
~JONATHAN CLEMENTS

CAN YOU AFFORD TO RETIRE?

IMPORTANT IDEAS

KEY CHAPTER TAKEAWAYS—SUMMARY

IN CHAPTER THREE, WE LEARNED:

● Establishing your financial readiness to retire is a process, and involves a number of moving parts. But it isn't as difficult as many people think.

● It's wise to be *conservative* when factoring the *income* you think you'll be able to generate—and *liberal* when calculating your anticipated *expenses*.

● You can view your financial readiness to retire based how much you'll *need* or on how much you *have*. Which basis you use depends whether you've got time yet, or are at retirement's doorstep.

● At this stage you need to calculate three things: *anticipated expenses*, *anticipated fixed income*, and *assets*. (This chapter of the workbook is designed to help you coordinate this.)

● If your calculations show that you are falling short, don't panic. There may be a number of things you can do strategically to improve your situation, especially if you have a little time before retirement.

● For risk management, *tactical asset management* is an approach I believe is far superior to the classic (and volatile) "buy and hold asset allocation" model. Tactical asset management prioritizes protection from downside risk. It emphasizes monitoring and flexibility, strives at all times to keep your money out of harm's way in bad times, and seeks to grow your money when opportunity presents itself.

HOW DO I MAKE THE MOST OF
THIS CHAPTER'S ESSENTIALS?

We'll use some worksheets to assemble key lists and make sure you include all the important pieces. We'll calculate:
- what you anticipate your expenses to be
- what you know your fixed income will be, and
- an accurate list of your assets.

Then you will subtract your fixed income from your anticipated annual expenses and determine if you have enough money to retire. If it appears that you don't, we'll look at a checklist of some steps to take.

1. Calculate your expenses.

Projecting future expenses can be the least exact aspect of this process. There are many different ideas about formulas for coming up with a number, such as a percentage of your current expenses (anywhere from 50% to 100%) or "the 25 times" rule (in which, theoretically, if your nest egg is 25 times your annual expenses, you can safely draw 4% a year). I prefer to actually start with a list of specific expenses.

On the next page is a worksheet you can use to jog your awareness of typical as well as unique expenses, and fill in your projections. Not all may apply to you, but fill in as many as you know.

If you are married, be sure to include totals for both yourself and spouse where applicable (e.g., insurance premiums, healthcare expenses, cell phones, etc.).

EXPENSES (MONTHLY)

Food	_____
Power (Electric, Gas, Oil, Solar, etc.)	_____
Housing (Rent or mortgage)	_____
Property taxes	_____
Income taxes	_____
HOA fees	_____
Trash and recycling	_____
Pet food and health care	_____
Auto payment(s)	_____
Auto insurance	_____
Homeowner's/renter's insurance	_____
Life insurance	_____
Long-term care insurance	_____
Medicare supplemental plan	_____
Vitamins and supplements	_____
Internet	_____
Cable	_____
Cellular	_____
Food	_____
Gasoline	_____
Medications	_____
Medicare co-pays	_____
Uncovered medical expenses	_____
Legal	_____
Financial advisor	_____
Home maintenance	_____
Entertainment	_____
Travel	_____
Clothing	_____
Gifts	_____
Postage	_____
Banking fees	_____
Unique to me: _____	_____
Unique to me: _____	_____
Unique to me: _____	_____
Unforeseen expenses	_____

TOTAL ESTIMATED EXPENSES _____   **x 3%** (per year cost-of-living adjustment)*

TOTAL ADJUSTED EXPENSES _____

Some years will be more, some less; this serves as an average.

2. Calculate your fixed income.

Now add up all of your guaranteed fixed income—pensions, Social Security, and any other fixed income. Calculate on a monthly basis, for comparison to monthly expenses.

PENSION *(does not include IRAs or 401(k)s)*   _____

PENSION *(second spouse, if applicable)*   _____

*(See **CHAPTER 3** of *Retirement Planning Made Easy* for detailed information on monthly options that may be available to you; consult your employer/pension statement for specific amounts/options, and your retirement planning advisor for help choosing your best option. This figure may change depending on your choice.)

SOCIAL SECURITY

SPOUSE 1

Monthly benefit at age 62   _____

Monthly benefit at FULL retirement age   _____

Monthly benefit at age 70   _____

SPOUSE 2

Monthly benefit at age 62   _____

Monthly benefit at FULL retirement age   _____

Monthly benefit at age 70   _____

*The actual monthly amount you receive will depend on when you file. CHOOSE ONE for your income total. See **CHAPTER 9** of this workbook and of the companion book *Retirement Planning Made Easy* for detailed information on strategies for maximizing Social Security that may apply to you. As discussed in the book several times, be sure to get a Social Security analysis from a qualified advisor to determine your best option.)

OTHER SOURCES OF FIXED INCOME (SUCH AS RENTAL INCOME)

Rental income   _____

Other source   _____

Other source   _____

Other source   _____

TOTAL FIXED INCOME   _____

(this amount should include only ONE Social Security amount based on retirement age)

3. Subtract income from expenses.

Now you have an idea of what your annual expenses will be, with cost-of-living adjustments added in. You know what your guaranteed fixed income is. Now you can deduct your income from your expenses and find out where you stand (you can calculate monthly, annually, or both). Your advisor will help you use these totals to devise a plan.

	MONTHLY	ANNUALLY
ALL FIXED INCOME:	_____	_____
ESTIMATED EXPENSES:	_____	_____
EXCESS (IF ANY) **+**	_____	_____
SHORTFALL (IF ANY) **-**	_____	_____

EXAMPLE: if your estimated annual expenses are $50,000 and your estimated fixed income is $38,000, you have a $12,000 shortfall—or about $1000 a month you will need to make up.

CAN YOU AFFORD TO RETIRE?

THINK ABOUT...

SETTING ASIDE AN EMERGENCY FUND FROM ASSETS
I *highly* recommend you create a separate account that you do NOT include in your withdrawal calculations. It can be invested and growing. This money would keep you from reducing your core portfolio (and therefore income) in emergencies. If you create an emergency fund, be sure to reduce the assets column by this amount accordingly.

4. Calculate your assets.

Here we will list assets that can be used to generate additional income to help make up any shortfall between your fixed income and your expenses. Additionally, the strategies listed on the next page can help reduce the gap.

SAVINGS IN TAXABLE RETIREMENT ACCOUNTS: IRA and 401(k)

401(k) (yours) _____

401(k) (spouse) _____

IRA (yours) _____

IRA (spouse) _____

Roth IRA _____

*Remember, since you haven't paid the taxes on this money yet—except for Roth IRA—state and federal taxes will substantially reduce these monies at the time of withdrawal. Specific tax strategies can help, but the totals you see in your accounts now will generally be taxed at your then-current tax rate (both state and federal) once you begin taking withdrawals. See CHAPTER 6 of *Retirement Planning Made Easy* for more on IRAs and 401(ks).

ALL OTHER SAVINGS

Certificates of Deposit _____

Brokerage Account 1 _____

Brokerage Account 2 _____

Annuities _____

Interest Savings Account 1 _____

Interest Savings Account 2 _____

Bonds _____

REAL ESTATE AND HARD ASSETS THAT MAY BE SOLD/INVESTED

Property _____

Hard Asset _____

Other Asset _____

TOTAL ASSET VALUES _____

5. Strategies for a shortfall...

Don't panic. It happens to a lot of people—and there may be time to amend or ways to adjust. Explore these possibilities with your advisor and your family:

❏ **Have all of your calculations have been done correctly?** Sometimes you can draw income from certain areas, or at specific times, to help you increase income in your front years of retirement (years 1 through 5) while allowing years 6 through 10 and years 11 through 16 (and so on) to grow to acceptable levels safely. Ask your qualified advisor about designing a plan to do this.

NOTES:

_____
_____
_____

❏ **Are you still a few years away from your desired date?** Consider increasing your savings. Small sacrifices today can go a long way in retirement.

NOTES:

_____
_____
_____

❏ **Take a closer look at the expenses you decided on.** Are there areas where you can cut back?

NOTES:

_____
_____
_____

❏ **Delay retirement.** Continue to work for a few more years. This will allow you to continue saving, as well as allow your assets to continue to grow before you start taking withdrawals.

NOTES:

_____
_____
_____

THINK ABOUT...

❏ **Consider cutting back your hours if possible, rather than fully retiring (at this time).** You can be "semi-retired." You may be able to draw on Social Security, or your spouse may be able to draw on the spousal benefit under Social Security, to make up the difference from your scaled-back hours. You can still leave your assets to grow. (See Chapter 9 of *Retirement Planning Made Easy* for more on Social Security strategies.)

NOTES:

_____

_____

_____

❏ **Consider downsizing.** If you own a big house with a big tax bill and expensive utilities, you might consider selling your home—either while still working, or as soon as you retire.

NOTES:

_____

_____

_____

❏ **Will you be moving to a new area that is less expensive then where you are now?** Make sure you base your expenses on the cost of living there. This could put you right where you need to be financially. If that wasn't the plan, consider doing so.

NOTES:

_____

_____

_____

❏ **Are your children living with you and not contributing?** Maybe it's time!

NOTES:

_____

_____

_____

PREPARING FOR STRATEGY SESSIONS

KEY CHAPTER TAKEAWAYS—SUMMARY

IN CHAPTER FOUR, WE LEARNED:

- A lot of advisors will give you a "free consultation"; that's a great way to get a feel for someone's skills and knowledge, and your compatibility. But it's *not* a great way to get your retirement planning done. Limiting yourself to just one free conversation may *cost* you money, not save it— because you're missing out on all the deep planning that yields a low-risk, low-volatility, solid retirement income plan. If you don't engage in strategy sessions with an advisor, you may lose money in the long run.

- Within 30 minutes of a free consultation, you're likely to have a feel for whether this advisor is a good fit for what you want to accomplish. This will be especially true if you've done your homework in advance and know what you need and are looking for. Having a general outline before you begin gives you a place to start and an idea of where you want to end up. It will also keep you on track and focused.

- If the first consultation is productive, it *can* serve as your first strategy session. The first strategy session should consist of a series of questions and answers, along with gathering of information.

- Successive strategy sessions should consist of a recap of your last meeting plus discussion of any analysis that has been completed, and proposed ideas for your consideration. It helps to be open to new ideas and ask questions. Make sure that you have input. Don't be intimidated.

- Having all the necessary documents accessible helps your advisor to do his or her job well. Gather the relevant information you need before the meeting. Use the checklists in this workbook chapter.

HOW DO I MAKE THE MOST OF THIS CHAPTER'S ESSENTIALS?

We'll use:

- A checklist to make sure you gather all the important material for your first session with an advisor

- A questionnaire to help you develop a written vision outlining where you want to be in retirement, in every sense.

- A checklist to make sure your strategy sessions are proceeding through each stage with the correct steps being taken.

1. Gather your material.

Gathering the relevant financial information, as discussed earlier, is key to preparing for the first strategy session. Bringing this workbook with all of the questions you've answered so far, and lists and calculations you've made, will also be extremely helpful.

STATEMENT AND CONTRACTS TO BRING

Check these items off and organize them in a folder or envelope.
Bring them along with your workbook (with as much filled out as you can).

- ❏ At least two prior years' tax returns
- ❏ Social Security statements (www.ssa.gov)
- ❏ Brokerage statements
- ❏ Annuity and life insurance contracts
- ❏ 401(k), IRA and pension statements
- ❏ Estate planning documents (Chapter 7 of this workbook should also be filled out)
- ❏ Advisor's completed questionnaire, if requested

In addition to the separate statements and documents listed on the previous page, you'll want to bring the following information. You can organize it by filling it all in here so that you have it all in one place when you bring your workbook—or if this information is documented elsewhere, you can bring those papers in their existing forms.

Even if you choose to fill in data here, you may also want to bring related and supporting documents.

STATEMENT AND CONTRACTS TO BRING

❏ BENEFICIARY DESIGNATIONS

Life insurance beneficiary(ies) _____

IRA beneficiary(ies) _____

401(k) beneficiary(ies) _____

Savings/CD account beneficiary (ies) _____

OTHER _____

OTHER _____

❏ EXISTING DEBT INFORMATION

Owed on credit cards   _____

Owed on mortgage   _____

Owed on car(s)   _____

Owed on other loans   _____

Other lines of credit   _____

❏ INFORMATION ON REAL ESTATE OWNED

NOTE FOR EACH:
▶ How it is titled?
   (Joint tenants in common, joint tenants with right of survivorship, life estate deed, individual, in trust?)
▶ Do you plan to sell it, rent it, or stay in it?
▶ Will rental generate income? Will sale generate cash assets?

PROPERTY 1: _____

PROPERTY 2: _____

PROPERTY 3: _____

PROPERTY 4: _____

❏ Preliminary budget information (Use Chapter 2 of this workbook)

❏ Hard asset values list (with estimated values)

You will want to include jewelry, stamp collections, art, antiques, high-value vehicles and other enduring assets.

_____ $ _____   _____ $ _____

_____ $ _____   _____ $ _____

_____ $ _____   _____ $ _____

_____ $ _____   _____ $ _____

_____ $ _____   _____ $ _____

❏ A list of questions you would like answers to

FOR EXAMPLE:
▌ What is your area of expertise? Accumulation? Distribution? Anything else?
▌ What is the average age of your clientele? *(if not 50 or above, likely minimal or no distribution planning experience)*
▌ Do you work under the fiduciary standard?
▌ Do you design income plans that cover 25-plus years of retirement?
▌ Do you offer a factual Social Security analysis report?
▌ Does the income plan include long-term care planning?
▌ Does the income plan include any estate planning strategies? Do you work with an attorney for estate planning needs?
▌ Do you know how to analyze and compare life insurance?
▌ Do you do an expense assessment?
▌ How do you determine a client's risk tolerance?
▌ Can you help with Medicare supplemental plan choices?
▌ Do you work with an accountant ?
▌ Do you keep up on public policy and legal changes? Will I be informed of changes that may affect my plan?
▌ How did your client portfolios do in 2008 when the stock market crashed? If they lost more than 10%, what is your answer as to why? *(If they say "everyone lost money," then they probably have no idea why.)*
▌ Do you use a one-size-fits-all model?
▌ Do you plan for inflation? What percentage do you use?
▌ How often do you meet for review?
▌ How often do you monitor the progress of my plan?
▌ What makes you different from other advisors?

_____

_____

_____

_____

_____

_____

_____

_____

_____

2. Create an outline of your vision.

Let's build a preliminary map and guidance tool to give your advisor (and you!) a better idea of what you want your retirement to look like and what you want to accomplish.

You probably know what you want your retirement to look like. You've had years to think about it: what you want to do, where you want to live, vacations you want to take, volunteer work you want to do. You may have also thought about the obstacles that might arise, and the money you think you'll need.

Write it all down, including a wish list. It's a place to begin, whether or not it is all ultimately achievable.

WHERE I WANT TO BE AND WHAT I WANT TO DO

In my retirement, I want to:

...live in a home that *(describe size, style, features):*

_____

_____

...live in [town(s), state(s), country/countries]:

_____

_____

...travel to/visit:

_____

_____

_____

...learn to/study:

_____

_____

_____

...contribute to:

_____

_____

_____

...volunteer at/with:

_____

_____

_____

...practice sports like:

_____

_____

_____

OTHER THINGS I WANT FOR MY RETIREMENT

_____

_____

_____

_____

_____

_____

3. Strategy Sessions—Steps & Stages

Use this checklist to make sure your strategy sessions with your advisor are on target, focused, moving through a logical process, and meeting your needs.

A. THE INITIAL STRATEGY SESSION

A productive first consultation can serve as your first strategy session. Your advisor should ask questions and gather information. Check off as follows:

❏ Advisor asked about my income needs

❏ Advisor asked about fixed income I will be able to count on

❏ Advisor educated me about risk tolerance and assessed mine.

❏ Advisor took my Social Security information to conduct a comprehensive "best option" analysis

❏ Advisor took my pension information to conduct a comprehensive "best option" analysis

❏ Advisor asked for tax returns in order to conduct tax planning strategies

❏ Advisor asked for life insurance and long-term care contracts (if any)

❏ Advisor answered all my questions competently and respectfully

B. SUCCESSIVE STRATEGY SESSIONS

How many times you meet with an advisor will depend on how much work needs to be done. It can be as few as three, with as many as four or five initially. Make sure the following is covered over these sessions:

❏ A recap of first session, including needs, goals, and assessed risk tolerance

❏ A discussion of my current portfolio and how it fits into my retirement goals

❏ A discussion of proposed changes to current portfolio, with reasons

❏ My Social Security claiming strategy, with analysis explained

❏ My pension options, with analysis explained

❏ A discussion of income/asset protection strategies

❐ Review of initial draft of my income plan and its design, including pros and cons and risk management features

❐ Proposed monitoring

❐ Future adjustments that may be needed

❐ All my questions have been answered and concerns addressed

❐ I have had input and do not feel confused or intimidated

B. IMPLEMENTATION

Only when you are comfortable with the projected outcomes and results, and have a clear understanding of what has been designed to achieve them, should you move forward and start the process of implementation. How long this takes will depend on how many moving parts there are.

❐ I am comfortable with the projected outcomes and results

❐ I fully understand the plan that has been designed to achieve the results

NOTES

_____

_____

_____

_____

_____

_____

_____

MONEY IS ONLY A TOOL. IT WILL TAKE YOU WHEREVER YOU WISH, BUT IT WILL NOT REPLACE YOU AS THE DRIVER.
~AYN RAND

A PLAN WITH A PURPOSE

KEY CHAPTER TAKEAWAYS—SUMMARY

IN CHAPTER FIVE, WE LEARNED:

● Modern portfolio theory emphasizes "diversification" as the key to all investing, but this alone does not protect the safety of retirement income. I favor an investing style called "*tactical asset management*"—a dynamic investment strategy that actively adjusts a portfolio's asset allocation.

● To help minimize losses in your portfolio, it must be monitored and flexibly positioned so you can go into a "risk off" (cash) position quickly when necessary.

● In retirement, cash *flow* is king; disbursement strategy is at least as key as your total assets. Without the right disbursement strategy, spending can happen too quickly, or overzealous caution can over-restrict your retired life. Either way, your money is then controlling you. The key is *balance*.

● Your income plan is a roadmap or blueprint that will create balance for you. Done right, it offers a "permission slip" to live comfortably, within your means and without worry.

● Your strategy's central objective should be reliable, inflation-adjusted income that lasts through retirement. That creates a "strong probability" blueprint (a plan with a high probability of long-term success). The critical "ROI" here is *Reliability Of Income*, NOT Return On Investment.

● With a Reliability of Income (ROI) blueprint, we use a disbursement strategy that divides your capital into six segments of five years each. This strategy gives you a 20- to 30-year forward view of your retirement.

HOW DO I MAKE THE MOST OF
THIS CHAPTER'S ESSENTIALS?

● Use this chapter to familiarize yourself with the segmented Reliability of Income strategy mentioned in the last bullet on the previous page.

● If your advisor is not familiar with and does not use such a strategy, you may want to share this outline with him or her, and ask for a comparison of the recommended strategy to this one. What is the reasoning behind the advisor's preference for a different plan design vs this one? (There may be good reasons— just make sure you understand them and agree.)

● The sample blueprint in this chapter sets up the basic structure of the strategy. You can fill in specific numbers on your own or with the help of your advisor, and play with it to get a feel for how it would yield.

THINK ABOUT...

1. The ROI Blueprint: 25-Year View

This highly efficient strategy gives you a 20- to 30-year forward view of your retirement. For this example, we'll use a 25-year view, since most retire at 65 and looking ahead 25 years brings you to age 90. We'll look at what happens after 90, too.

This strategy sets up six segments. Each of the first five segments represents five years. These segments are designed to generate a reliable monthly income for the first 25 years, with a cost-of-living increase every five years. (To provide a cost-of-living increase more often is possible, but requires more assets or a higher rate of return.)

The blueprint on the next page shows the basic structure for this strategy; the specific amount of assets allocated to each segment will depend on your individual situation. But the concept remains the same: the amount allocated to each segment becomes progressively smaller as we move out in time. And the further out a segment is, the more aggressive the investment can be.

No matter where you are in the 25 years, tactical asset management remains vital— measures must be taken to minimize drawdown within every segment.

REMEMBER:

▶ The amount allocated to each segment becomes progressively smaller the further we get from the start date.

▶ The further out a segment is, the more aggressive the investment can be.

SEGMENT 1

The most conservative, since you will be using this to generate your monthly income in the first five years. This needs to be the largest allocation for that reason as well.

SEGMENT 2

Has already been invested for five years, growing.
It can be a little less money and a little more aggressive.

SEGMENT 3

Has now been invested for 10 years, growing.
It can be an even smaller amount, and more aggressive still.

SEGMENT 4

Has now been invested for 15 years, growing.
You have time before you tap this, so it can be another degree of aggressive.

SEGMENT 5

Has now been invested for 20 years, growing.
With two decades before you're into this cash, you can be the most aggressive.

SEGMENT 6

Assuming you made it this far, congratulations—you are now 90 years old!
The goal of Segment 6 is to provide additional income should you live beyond this age, and/or to leave an inheritance to your heirs.
This segment has now been invested for 25 years, growing and waiting for you.

SEGMENT 7 - OPTIONAL

You may also want to consider one additional segment for anticipated or unanticipated large purchases.

SEGMENT 1

$ _____ Invested in: _____ at _____% yield

$ _____ Invested in: _____ at _____% yield

SEGMENT 2

$ _____ Invested in: _____ at _____% yield

$ _____ Invested in: _____ at _____% yield

SEGMENT 3

$ _____ Invested in: _____ at _____% yield

$ _____ Invested in: _____ at _____% yield

SEGMENT 4

$ _____ Invested in: _____ at _____% yield

$ _____ Invested in: _____ at _____% yield

SEGMENT 5

$ _____ Invested in: _____ at _____% yield

$ _____ Invested in: _____ at _____% yield

SEGMENT 6

$ _____ Invested in: _____ at _____% yield

$ _____ Invested in: _____ at _____% yield

SEGMENT 7 - OPTIONAL

$ _____ Invested in: _____ at _____% yield

$ _____ Invested in: _____ at _____% yield

TOTAL INVESTED _____

NOTE: This model can be extremely productive, but many people will find it too hard to sort out and implement by themselves. If that includes you, you're not alone! The above model illustrates how it works, but filling it in properly is where your financial planning expert can help. I offer an income planning educational site where you can further educate yourself and also inquire about having this done for you. You can contact me directly from the website. Just go to www.dmarra. incomeforlifemodel.com (or go to www.marrafinancialgroup.com and link over by clicking on "Retirement Time" under Helpful Resources at the bottom of my website's main page.)

CHAPTER SIX

401(K) AND IRA ROLLOVERS

KEY CHAPTER TAKEAWAYS—SUMMARY

IN CHAPTER SIX, WE LEARNED:

- A "qualified" plan is a retirement plan that qualifies for four tax benefits when it meets certain IRS code requirements and ERISA requirements: Employers can deduct allowable contributions in the year they made contributions on your behalf; the participant can exclude contributions and earnings from taxable income until withdrawal at retirement; earnings on the funds held by the plan's trust are not taxed to that trust, and usually, you and subsequently your beneficiaries can continue to delay taxation of these funds by transferring them to another tax-deferred arrangement, such as an IRA. (Please see the companion book *Retirement Planning Made Easy* for more in-depth information.)

- Qualified retirement plans fall into three general categories: A *defined benefit plan* ("traditional" company pension plan where the retirement benefit is definite); a *defined contribution plan* (the contribution to the plan is defined, but the benefit paid is not defined and is determined by amount contributed and performance of investment) and *cash balance* or other hybrid plans (these offer elements of both defined benefit and defined contribution plans). (Please see the companion book *Retirement Planning Made Easy* for more in-depth information.)

- A 401(k) is a traditional, employer-sponsored retirement plan that is outlined in IRS tax code section 401(k). Your money is invested before tax and grows on a tax-deferred basis. The tax is not paid until you begin withdrawing from the account.

- An Individual Retirement Account (IRA) is an account that you set up on an individual basis, rather than through an employer. The money you deposit is tax-deductible and the earnings are tax-deferred. When you later begin withdrawing money, every dollar is taxable at your then-current tax rate.

- A Roth IRA is a type of Individual Retirement Account in which you deposit money on an "after-tax" basis rather then pre-tax. You cannot use the deposit as a tax deduction on your tax return, but the benefit is that when you do begin taking withdrawals, every dollar is completely free from taxation at both the federal and state level. Also, you never *have* to take distributions and can pass the entire account on to heirs, at which point tax-free distributions must begin. With a traditional IRA, you must begin withdrawals at age 70-½ or face heavy penalties.

- A rollover is the act of taking a distribution from one retirement plan—a 401(k) or other tax-qualified plan—and moving it into a new plan. As an exception to the rule of taxable distributions: while being moved, the funds will not be taxed until a future taxable distribution, as long as certain rules are met.

- There is a lot to learn about doing a rollover properly for a successful outcome—and that is what the rest of Chapter 6 in *Retirement Planning Made Easy* covers. There are a number of procedures available when you are ready to proceed with a rollover (these include direct rollovers, trustee-to-trustee transfers, and 60-day rollover). The right one will depend on your age; the type of plan you're moving from and moving to; your goals; and other factors. Get advice if you're unsure.

 THINK ABOUT...

HOW DO I MAKE THE MOST OF THIS CHAPTER'S ESSENTIALS?

With IRAs and 401(k)s, the most important thing is to understand your specific plan type(s) and what strategies apply that will best serve your goals. Simply learning all you can and then consulting an advisor is best. Be sure to write down all of your questions about any qualified plans to bring to your advisor.

ESTATE PLANNING

KEY CHAPTER TAKEAWAYS—SUMMARY

IN CHAPTER SEVEN, WE LEARNED:

- Estate Planning offers you the opportunity to help control how your estate is taxed, how it is managed, and how it distributed.

- Professional expertise in estate planning can reveal opportunities you may not be aware of that can save you and your family money and hassle. If you don't learn about these, you may give the government, courts, and attorneys money that could have gone to your loved ones. You should hire an estate-planning attorney to have your plan prepared.

- If you procrastinate or avoid this planning, you risk leaving a mess behind for loved ones, and not having your wishes carried out regarding finances or your own medical care.

- No estate is too small to plan for. Younger people may have less to arrange than older people with larger families and financial complexities, but everyone has an estate.

- Your estate plan must be kept current; have it reviewed every three to five years, as well as after any life-changing events.

- Do your part: professional advice and assistance is essential to take advantage of all opportunities and save your loved ones money and grief. However, there is a great deal for *you* to prepare, decide, and think about in order to facilitate the process. This workbook chapter will help you consider all of the vital questions and gather all of the important material.

HOW DO I MAKE THE MOST OF THIS CHAPTER'S ESSENTIALS?

- Use this chapter to prompt yourself to think about and answer all the important questions related to your estate. There will also be places to fill in the information you gather and document your decisions.

- The following pages will help you consider and determine: who to include in your estate; your assets and liabilities; who will make medical decisions for you and who will act as your executor; your preferred funeral arrangements; and contacts and digital assets you should record.

- Also included is a checklist for finding an estate planning attorney (who will likely be impressed at all of your preparation if you use this workbook!) and a checklist for keeping your plan current.

- You may also share this information with your retirement income planning advisor. Your personal goals and wishes can help inform how your income strategy and distribution is designed, so it's helpful for your advisor to be aware of them.

INFO TO GATHER

1. Assets and Who Gets What

Here is where you can inventory major assets. Include real estate and how it's titled; bank accounts; brokerage accounts; 401(k)s, IRAs, life insurance policies, and hard assets. You'll want to list where the account is held, the account numbers, and beneficiaries if already designated. (Check and confirm your beneficiary designations. Do any of the accounts have a transfer on death/due upon death with beneficiaries named?)

Other assets include cars, boats, jewelry, artwork, collections, digital assets such as websites, and furniture, just to name a few.

Start by listing assets on the next few pages; then you can go back and list benefiaries as step two.

ASSET	LOCATION & ACCOUNT #	BENEFICIARY	ALREADY DESIGNATED?
			☐
			☐
			☐
			☐
			☐
			☐
			☐

ASSET	LOCATION & ACCOUNT #	BENEFICIARY	ALREADY DESIGNATED?
			☐
			☐
			☐
			☐
			☐
			☐
			☐

ASSET	LOCATION & ACCOUNT #	BENEFICIARY	ALREADY DESIGNATED?
			☐
			☐
			☐
			☐
			☐
			☐
			☐

ASSET	LOCATION & ACCOUNT #	BENEFICIARY	ALREADY DESIGNATED?
_____	_____	_____	☐
_____	_____	_____	
_____	_____	_____	☐
_____	_____	_____	
_____	_____	_____	☐
_____	_____	_____	
_____	_____	_____	☐
_____	_____	_____	
_____	_____	_____	☐
_____	_____	_____	
_____	_____	_____	☐
_____	_____	_____	
_____	_____	_____	☐
_____	_____	_____	

THINGS TO DO

MAKE EXTRA COPIES IF YOU NEED TO LIST MORE ASSETS THAN THESE PAGES ALLOW
You can tuck them into the workbook or bring them along in a folder with statements and other separate materials.

2. Who to Include

Now go back over the last few pages of listed assets, and write in the names of the people who should receive each asset.

Divorces, multiple marriages, stepchildren, step-grandchildren, and so on can complicate estate planning. You may or may not wish to include all members of a blended, extended family.

It might help to make a *general* list of all chosen benefactors below, to be able to see the big picture, before you assign specific assets (on previous pages).

_____ _____

_____ _____

_____ _____

_____ _____

_____ _____

_____ _____

_____ _____

_____ _____

EXECUTOR _____

CONTACT INFORMATION _____

When choosing an executor or trustee, think about personalities, family dynamics, and skill with handling money. Choose someone competent with attention to detail.

A COPY OF MY WILL IS LOCATED AT: _____

ATTORNEY NAME AND PHONE: _____

Some recipients may need stipulations on distributions (underage children, aging parents, etc.)

RECIPIENTS WHO NEED TRUSTS OR DISTRIBUTIONS

_____

_____

_____

_____

_____

TRUSTEE _____

Trusts are an intricate subject about which entire books are written. The more assets you have, the more helpful a trust can become. Assets that already have named beneficiaries, however, do not need to be titled inside a trust.

EXECUTORS, TRUSTEES, AND ATTORNEYS-IN-FACT

These are enormous responsibilities, so choose wisely. Be sure to have a conversation with the people you choose, and make sure they're comfortable handling these responsibilities. Have a contingency list in place as well, in case your first choices are unable to perform their functions when the time comes.

3. Liabilities

INFO TO GATHER

List any liabilities that you have.
Are there existing loans or other debts that will need to be settled?

LOAN/DEBT NAME/TYPE	AMOUNT	INSTITUTION ACCT #

4. Who Will Make Medical Decisions

Please see the companion book *Retirement Planning Made Easy* for more in-depth information on all of these types of directives. These can be prepared by an attorney, or you can get the appropriate forms for these directives on the Internet or from your legal or planning advisors. Fill them out; then indicate that you have done so and where you keep them. I favor preparation by a qualified attorney.

Basic documents you should consider having are:

POWER OF ATTORNEY (GENERAL / DURABLE / SPRINGING)

A *General* POA gives your attorney-in-fact (person you designate) the same power that you yourself have—such as the power to sign documents and conduct financial transactions on your behalf. These POAs may be rescinded, and end upon your incapacitation or death.

A *Durable* POA remains in effect even after you become incapacitated. Without this, if you do become incapacitated, no one can represent you in court unless and until a conservator or guardian is appointed by the court. These can also be rescinded prior to incapacitation and can remain in effect until your death.

A *Springing* POA allows your attorney-in-fact to act for you IF you become incapacitated and does not become effective *until* you are incapacitated.

❑ **MY POA IS COMPLETE AND STORED:** _____

MY ATTORNEY IN FACT IS: _____

MEDICAL POWER OF ATTORNEY / HEALTHCARE PROXY

Authorize someone you trust to be your healthcare agent to make medical decisions for you when you are unable to make them for yourself.

❑ **MY MEDICAL POA IS COMPLETE AND STORED:** _____

MY ATTORNEY IN FACT IS: _____

LIVING WILL

This is also known as your *advanced medical directive*, a *patient advocate designation*, or an *advanced directive*. This document spells out how you should be cared for in an emergency when you cannot speak for yourself or you are incapacitated for any other reason. It covers desired quality of life and end-of-life treatments, including treatments you do *not* want. It also covers resuscitation. It provides a way to "speak" with the doctor who is caring for you when you cannot, and advises him/her about how to approach your care and treatment. You should be as specific as possible within this document about your wishes.

❑ **MY LIVING WILL IS COMPLETE AND STORED:** _____

5. Funeral Arrangements

You can state your desire to be buried or cremated, along with any other express wishes. This should also be discussed with your family or the person(s) who will take care of your burial prior to your death. It's possible that they won't read or be aware of this document until it's too late, although it's best if you *do* share this information in advance. You do not need an attorney for this.

I want to be: _____ BURIED _____ CREMATED

I would like to be buried at (list cemetery name, address, phone number and plot information if available) _____
_____
_____
_____

I have prepaid: _____ BURIAL (at : _____)

_____ CREMATION SERVICES (at: _____)

_____ FUNERAL SERVICES (at: _____)

_____ RECEPTION (at: _____)

_____ OTHER (at: _____)

Proof of purchase/information is located: _____
_____
_____

Burial information is held by (*name and contact info of relative or friend):*
_____
_____

If **cremated**, I would like ashes to be kept or scattered in the following way by the following person(s): _____
_____
_____
_____
_____
_____

THINK ABOUT...

MY FUNERAL, SERVICE AND/OR RECEPTION

Use the space below to list any and all pertinent information you would like your loved ones to have about your wishes for a service, funeral, or party.

When listing people involved, include contact info wherever possible.

Be sure to include any details that apply or matter to you about:

✔ LOCATION	✔ INVITEES	✔ FLOWERS
✔ OFFICIANT(S)	✔ PALLBEARERS	✔ FOODS
✔ MUSICAL SELECTIONS	✔ WHO WILL PLAY/SING	✔ DONATIONS
✔ POEMS OR READINGS	✔ WHO WILL READ	✔ CASKET

_____

_____

_____

_____

_____

_____

_____

_____

_____

_____

_____

_____

_____

_____

_____

_____

_____

_____

_____

_____

6. Contacts (Miscellaneous)

List here all of the people who should be contacted in the event that you are incapacitated or upon your death.

NAME	PHONE	EMAIL	CITY

THINGS TO DO

MAKE EXTRA COPIES IF YOU NEED TO LIST MORE ASSETS THAN THIS PAGE ALLOWS
You can tuck them into the workbook or bring them along in a folder with statements and other separate materials.

7. Digital Assets and Passwords

Fill in everything that's applicable.

WEBSITE(S) I OWN/OPERATE (URL/HOSTED AT)	USERNAME	PW

KEY WEBSITE(S)/ACCOUNTS TO ACCESS	USERNAME	PW

THINGS TO DO

MAKE EXTRA COPIES IF YOU NEED TO LIST
MORE THAN THESE PAGES ALLOW
You can tuck them into the workbook or bring them
along in a folder with statements and other separate
materials.

THINK ABOUT...

A MASTER PASSWORD PROGRAM

If you install a master password through one of these programs, then you only need to give your loved one(s) a single password that will allow access to all your other websites (instead of listing them all on paper or digitally).

You may also want to verbally give your "password keeper" the password rather than document it here. It's all about your comfort.

DIGITAL ASSETS AND PASSWORDS *CONTINUED*

KEY WEBSITE(S)/ACCOUNTS TO ACCESS	USERNAME	PW

8. Finding an Estate Planning Attorney

If this is the first time you're having an estate plan prepared, you'll need an attorney who specializes in estate planning. If you're updating an existing plan, you may want to consider using the attorney that created it. If you've already built a working relationship, it may only take a brief conversation over the phone or in person to facilitate changes.

If you've undergone significant personal or financial changes, or you feel you need a greater degree of sophistication, then consider making a change to obtain the level of expertise that your situation warrants.

CHECKLIST FOR FINDING A NEW ESTATE PLANNING ATTORNEY

❏ Ask your accountant or financial advisor (one you trust and have a relationship with) for a referral to an attorney used by other clients with comparable circumstances.

❏ Ask an attorney or two who you like and trust (even if their expertise lies in other legal areas).

❏ Martindale.com is a well-known nationwide directory that allows you to search in your specific location as well as in a particular area of practice.

❏ The American College of Trust and Estate Council's website (actec.org) notes that it elects members who demonstrate a high level of integrity, commitment, competence, and experience in the area of trusts and estates.

Once you have narrowed your choices down to two or three, call to set up consultations. You may be able to have the consultation via phone rather than face-to-face meeting, although meeting a prospective attorney in person can be very helpful.

After you've made your choice, gather everything you've put together (including everything you've put together using this chapter) and meet with your new attorney.

9. Keeping it Current

Estate planning is not something you do once and check off your to-do list. Many life events are significant and can affect your estate. Also, laws that can affect your estate change and evolve.

To keep your estate plan current, have it reviewed at least once every three to five years (more often in the event of significant life changes).

Here is a short list of events that may require you to update your plan:

❑ The birth of a child or grandchild

❑ The death of a spouse

❑ Death of a child or grandchild

❑ The sale or purchase of a home

❑ Serious illness

❑ Purchase of a business/sale of a business

❑ Significant increase or decrease in assets

❑ Change in marital status

❑ Death of other beneficiaries

❑ A move to a new state

❑ Relationship changes with beneficiaries or fiduciaries

❑ New tax laws

❑ New marriages

❑ Children reaching adult age

ANNUITIES

KEY CHAPTER TAKEAWAYS—SUMMARY

IN CHAPTER EIGHT, WE LEARNED:

● Annuities have received some bad press, but you need to consider the source and any inherent biases. Don't take everything you read and hear about annuities at face value. Apply your own due diligence as always and do some research.

● If guaranteed income is on your retirement income wish list, placing at least a portion of your money into annuities can be an excellent choice.

● There are many different types of annuities. It's important to understand the different types available to you and how one may benefit your situation over another. Especially relevant to your choice is which particular segment of your retirement you're trying to cover with your annuity.

● Annuities have limited liquidity during "surrender years" (the specified term during which you don't have access to the principal), so you should maintain liquid accounts outside an annuity.

● You can transfer money inside an annuity from one company to another without a tax penalty by performing what's known as a "1035 exchange."

● Guarantees are always based on the claims-paying ability of an insurance company. Most states have insurance guaranty associations that are governed by a board of directors and the state's insurance regulator. Guarantees can be as high as $500,000 in the event that an insurance company fails. However, no insurance companies failed in 2009 after the 2008 stock market crash—while 140 banks closed their doors.

HOW DO I MAKE THE MOST OF
THIS CHAPTER'S ESSENTIALS?

● Annuities are a complex subject; there are many different kinds that work in different ways, and there are different options for how to use them. There really are no quick tips or one-size-fits-all charts or worksheets that will apply to all annuities. The best thing you can do is educate yourself thoroughly—and it's worth doing.

● Use the companion to this workbook—the book *Retirement Planning Made Easy*—to learn the basics about annuities in greater detail. Also use recommended resources to conduct further research.

● Consult your retirement income planner with questions about annuities. If your retirement income planner doesn't know anything about them, and/or is excessivley negative about them without giving you clear and logical reasons, you may want to consult another professional for an unbiased opinion.

AMERICANS SHOULD CONSIDER PUTTING AS MUCH AS HALF OF THEIR ASSETS IN AN INCOME ANNUITY.
~GOVERNMENT ACCOUNTABILITY OFFICE

SOCIAL SECURITY

KEY CHAPTER TAKEAWAYS—SUMMARY

IN CHAPTER NINE, WE LEARNED:

● Social Security retirement benefits help provide lifetime, inflation-adjusted income. Coupled with retirement savings and any pension benefits you might receive, Social Security can serve as an important element of your retirement income.

● A well-thought-out strategy for claiming Social Security benefits can result in substantial additional retirement income. That's why you should hold off rushing to the Social Security office and signing papers as soon as you hit retirement. Instead, have a Social Security analysis done for you and learn about strategies that can increase your income substantially.

● Your monthly income from SS (*primary insurance amount*, or *PIA*) is based on your lifetime earnings, but it may be reduced based on when you claim benefits. You can claim benefits as early as 62, but you increase your benefits by 8 percent for every year you delay up till 70.

● When life expectancy was a little over 61, it made sense for some to begin collecting at age 62. But with a life expectancy for females of about 81 and for males of about 76, delaying can make financial sense in many cases.

● A strategy called "File and Suspend" can be highly lucrative for married couples. (See the companion book *Retirement Planning Made Easy* for details on how this works. This workbook chapter also lays out sample scenarios.)

● You can work in retirement and still receive Social Security, but benefits may be reduced until you reach full retirement age. The earnings could increase future benefits if they're higher than previously recorded earnings.

- Make sure your retirement income planner has a thorough understanding of different Social Security strategies, can offer you a detailed analysis, and explain the reasoning for your recommended strategy.

- In some cases, Social Security income may be taxable income. You may be able to strategically reduce taxation of Social Security, even if you fall into a base income bracket that makes your Social Security benefits taxable. You'll need to consult with a competent tax accountant.

HOW DO I MAKE THE MOST OF THIS CHAPTER'S ESSENTIALS?

- You can use this workbook chapter to view a sample scenario for "File and Suspend," to get a sense of how it works and whether it may apply to you.

- The taxation charts will help you gather the information you need to determine if your Social Security income might be taxable.

- Beyond this broad overview, Social Security benefit strategies depend on the individual and should be explored based on your unique situation. That's why you need to make sure that that your advisor knows how to strategize Social Security.

- Go to www.marrafinancialgroup.com and link over to my satellite Social Security educational website (called "Social Security Wise" listed under "Helpful Resources" at the bottom of the Home page) for further information, education and examples. Or go directly to www.dmarra.sswise.com.

- In addition, I offer a Social Security Strategy session that gives you a complete 22- to 27-page Social Security analysis based on your own personal situation, which will point you to your best claiming strategy. Just click on "Strategy Sessions" at www.marrafinancialgroup.com.

THINK ABOUT...

1. "File and Suspend"

Social Security rules provide that a spouse, whether or not he/she has ever worked, is entitled to a benefit equal to up to one-half of the other spouse's retirement benefit. This is called a *spousal benefit*.

A spouse cannot claim a spousal benefit unless and until the main beneficiary claims—*files* for—his/her benefit first. This doesn't mean that the main beneficiary must begin *taking* the benefits. A beneficiary can *file* for benefits at full retirement age —and then *immediately suspend receipt of* those benefits until a future date (like age 70). The spouse seeking the spousal benefit files a restricted application to receive a portion of the main beneficiary's benefit.

By suspending, the main beneficiary allows his or her benefit to grow at 8 percent per year in delayed retirement credits. Meanwhile, as a couple via the "auxiliary" spousal benefit, you get one-half of the main beneficiary's benefit until that time.

The spouse who filed the restricted application is also delaying his or her *own* benefit. So, while he or she receives half the main beneficiary's benefit, his or her own benefit also grows by 8 percent per year!

If done properly, this can result in tens of thousands of dollars over the lifetime of the two beneficiaries' benefits. It's complex to ensure that it's done right, as both beneficiaries have to handle the filing and the suspension in specific ways, and the exact strategy and total benefits paid depends on the age of each partner. See the companion book *Reitrement Planning Made Easy* for more detail, and be sure to discuss this with an experienced retirement income planner who's savvy about Social Security.

There are too many variables in the details of each situation to show specific results or amounts here—consult a professional for your analysis. However, the most basic structure of the process and its results are laid out on the next page.

Remember that I offer a detailed, comprehensive Social Security strategy session and analysis based on your situation and options. Go to www.marrafinancialgroup.com and link to my Social Security website, or go to www.dmarra.sswise.com.

You'll need to gather some basic info to get that analysis done, as shown on next page.

INFO TO GATHER

The basic information you'll need to know how File and Suspend would add up for you—and that you need for any Social Security scenario analysis—is right on your Social Security statement.

You'll need to know your benefit at minimum retirement age, full retirement age, and age 70.

FIRST SPOUSE

Monthly benefit at MINIMUM retirement age _____

Monthly benefit at FULL retirement age _____

Monthly benefit at AGE 70 _____

SECOND SPOUSE

Monthly benefit at MINIMUM retirement age _____

Monthly benefit at FULL retirement age _____

Monthly benefit at AGE 70 _____

POTENTIAL CHANGES TO FILE AND SUSPEND

A new bill has been proposed (at the time of this writing) that would significantly change the File and Suspend strategy with restricted application. If the bill is passed, which is likely, the proposed changes are as follows:

You would no longer be able to "file and suspend" for the purpose of triggering a benefit for your spouse. In order for a family member to claim a benefit on your Social Security record, you will have to be actually collecting your own benefit. With this change, there would be no benefits paid to anyone while your benefits are suspended.

You *would* still be able to file and suspend to allow your own benefits to grow by 8% per year until you are age 70. That will not change. But a spouse could no longer claim spousal benefits during that time.

If you turn 62 by December 31st, 2015, you would retain your right to collect a spousal benefit at your full retirement age. Anyone who is younger than 62 on that date will *not* be eligible to collect a spousal benefit. If you are entitled to both a retirement benefit based on your own earnings record, AND a spousal benefit because you're married (or divorced after at least 10 years of marriage) to someone who is eligible for benefits, you could receive only one of these—the higher of the two amounts.

That said, there remain hundreds of different scenarios to be addressed, and laws are always changing, so Social Security planning must continue to be a cornerstone in your retirement income planning.

2. Taxation of Social Security Benefits

Per the IRS, a quick way to find out if any of your benefits may be taxable is to add one-half of your annual Social Security benefits to all your other annual income, including interest and dividends, taxable pensions, investment income, wages and tax-exempt interest.

Next, compare this total to the base amounts below. If your total is more than the base amount for your filing status, then some of your benefits may be taxable. The base amounts are as shown on the next page, with space for totaling your income.

 INFO TO GATHER

A. SINGLE, HEAD OF HOUSEHOLD, QUALIFYING WIDOW OR WIDOWER WITH A DEPENDENT CHILD, OR MARRIED INDIVIDUALS FILING SEPARATELY WHO DID NOT LIVE WITH THEIR SPOUSES AT ANY TIME DURING THE YEAR

If all your income added together (along with half your Social Security income) is between $25,000 and $34,000, then up to 50% of your Social Security income may be taxable.

If all your income added together (along with half your Social Security income) is more than $34,000, up to 85% of your Social Security income may be taxable.

HALF YOUR SS INCOME   _____

ALL OTHER INCOME   _____ Use other worksheets from this workbook

TOTAL INCOME   _____ ❑ $25-34,000?   ❑ More than $34,000?

B. FOR MARRIED COUPLES FILING JOINTLY

If all your income added together (along with half your Social Security income) is between $32,000 and $44,000, then up to 50% of your Social Security income may be taxable.

If all your income added together (along with half your Social Security income) is more than $44,000, up to 85% of your Social Security income may be taxable.

HALF YOUR SS INCOME   _____

ALL OTHER INCOME   _____ Use other worksheets from this workbook

TOTAL INCOME   _____ ❑ $32-44,000?   ❑ More than $44,000?

Your base is $0.00—which means you will pay tax on 85% of your Social Security benefits if you have other income and use this filing status. You may want to consult with an accountant about possible financial planning and strategies to eliminate this tax burden even if you fall into one of these base income brackets.

WE PUT THOSE PAYROLL CONTRIBUTIONS THERE SO AS TO GIVE THE CONTRIBUTOR A LEGAL, MORAL AND POLITICAL RIGHT TO COLLECT THEIR PENSIONS AND THEIR UNEMPLOYMENT BENEFITS... NO DAMN POLITICIAN CAN EVER SCRAP MY SOCIAL SECURITY PROGRAM."

- FRANKLIN D. ROOSEVELT

LONG-TERM CARE

KEY CHAPTER TAKEAWAYS—SUMMARY

In Chapter TEN, we learned:

- Almost no one wants to talk about or think about long-term care, but with our aging population living longer and the increased risk of chronic diseases as we age, it's a topic we must confront.

- Many people are inclined to gamble that "it won't happen to them," but statistics suggest that during your retirement, you and/or your spouse are likely to need some kind of long-term care.

- Most people avoid long-term care coverage due to the sense that it's costly, but it is actually far more costly to pay for long-term care out of pocket if you need it than it is with a long-term care insurance policy.

- Besides cost, another deterrent for many people is the fear that they will never use the insurance. However, that doesnt stop most people from obtaining health, auto, life, or homeowner's insurance, and most people are glad they have those peace-of-mind protections even if they never file a claim.

- Insurance against a long-term care situation offers protection against your entire nest egg being decimated to pay for care at the end of your life.

HOW DO I MAKE THE MOST OF THIS CHAPTER'S ESSENTIALS?

- I recommend doing a little research on long-term care costs in your state and writing those numbers down. Spaces are provided. You'll have to do a little of your own legwork, but I think it'll be worth it.

- It's a good idea to review the statistics and be familiar with the probabilities. See the statistics in the book, and do some research on your own.

- Honestly assess your own health risks (individually and as a couple if you're married). Include health habits and family history.

- I recommend consulting a long-term care insurance agent or your advisor, and at least looking at costs vis-a-vis risks and your budget. There is no requirement to buy if you don't want to, but at least if you consider what the costs could be out of pocket and then look at the cost of insurance, you can make an informed decision.

1. Long-Term Care Costs in my State

Start at this site (you can find many other resources as well) and note the costs for each type of care in your state. http://longtermcare.gov/costs-how-to-pay/costs-of-care-in-your-state/

MEDIAN ANNUAL COST IN MY STATE FOR:		x 4%/year for _____ years*
Nursing Home Private Room	_____	_____
Nursing Home Semi-Private Room	_____	_____
Assisted Living Facility	_____	_____
Adult Day Health Care	_____	_____
Home Health Aide	_____	_____
Homemaker Services	_____	_____

Median annual nursing-home costs have increased 3.63% since 2011.
Choose and fill in an amount of time you might need LTC—and add about 4% a year for that many years.

How much time? According to 2004 data, the average length of stay for current nursing home residents is 835 days. Average length of stay for discharged residents is 270 days.

2. Protecting My Assets

The federal maximum community spouse resource allowance (amount you can keep and still receive Medicaid) is $119,220. The federal minimum community spouse resource allowance is $23,884. However, actual amounts vary by state. Check with your state's Medicaid agency to find out how much in resources you are allowed to keep if your spouse enters a nursing home.

My/our assets are worth: _____

- amount I am allowed to keep _____

Amount we would spend down _____

3. Compare to other insurance

OTHER INSURANCE I HOLD

	MONTHLY PREMIUM	ANNUAL PREMIUM	VALUE PROTECTED
HOME	_____	_____	_____
AUTO	_____	_____	_____
LIFE	_____	_____	_____
LTC	_____	_____	_____

4. Health status and long-term care risk

Many long-term care event stem from health conditions that are common in older Americans and that have known risk factors, whether lifestyle or hereditary. This form is by no means comprehensive, but it should get you thinking. Be honest!

CONDITION

	I HAVE LIFESTYLE FACTORS/HABITS ASSOCIATED WITH THIS CONDITION	I HAVE HAD THIS OR HAVE FAMILY HISTORY ASSOCIATED WITH THIS CONDITION
HEART DISEASE	☐ _____	☐ _____
STROKE	☐ _____	☐ _____
CANCER	☐ _____	☐ _____
DIABETES	☐ _____	☐ _____
DEMENTIA	☐ _____	☐ _____
BONE LOSS	☐ _____	☐ _____
LUNG DISEASE	☐ _____	☐ _____
ARTHRITIS	☐ _____	☐ _____
AUTOIMMUNE	☐ _____	☐ _____
OBESITY	☐ _____	☐ _____

NOTES

CPSIA information can be obtained
at www.ICGtesting.com
Printed in the USA
BVHW02s0132111018
529837BV00025B/1197/P

9 780997 221718